ONE PARENT, WHOLE FAMILY

ONE PARENT, WHOLE FAMILY

Building a Happy Home Solo

AVERY NIGHTINGALE

Creative Quill Press

CONTENTS

Contents

CHAPTER 1

Introduction

The study of the personal domestic organization of the one-mother family, apart from the important exceptions of the studies of Alexandra Riding, is truly scarce. It remains to be seen whether the practices of domestic organization of the one family have specific research characteristics, or not, with respect to the three essential aspects that define it - which stem from the subjective, not structural, experience of the family. Which cross-traffic, which organize, and to which Ramey soon refers, as additional hallmarks avoiding, arise those practices accidental. These attributes remind us of the temporality, meaning and practical regencia of the personal ensemble that generates an everyday family.

The desert motif is founded on Ramey's personal experience as a parent rearing her two sons alone in Los Angeles. She found that such childrearing was a difficult and oppressive experience to bear in the difficult mood of urbanization. The desert represents the place of isolation in which the mother finds herself less. However, Ramey expresses a certain sanguinity about urban experience - the desert for him seems to be a phenomenological core pitting that any parent, solo or partnered, can encounter within the home, for example, when it is felt that "there are dirty dishes, diapers, and dirty clothes everywhere." Perhaps Ramey's astoundingly high expectations of or possibly his practices of everyday housekeeping now appears to be somewhat conspicuous.

CHAPTER 2

Understanding the Challenges of Single Parenting

• Time management: You don't want to give up your job, but there is little time for one-on-one time with your children. In a traditional metrics, many feel that continuous work shifts lower the quality of life for lone parents. Families with only one father often have fewer assets. Also, children do better in families where parents have more resources, give more individual attention, and where there are fewer children. It may also be that everybody is too busy and wants to live beyond their own means. However, all families to a certain extent must deal with issues of time, finances, and general worries. Once you've created your schedule with your children and worked it out, don't refund it when last-minute invitations happen. Tell your children where you're going to be and who you're going to be with. Often you don't know why someone has sent an invitation to you at the last minute. Understand why, and if you think it makes sense with your schedule, you should take a better look at their individual request.

It's easy for parents who are on their own to feel ungrounded and unsure of their future. It may be easy to spend time thinking about what you didn't have when you were a child that would have made growing up better, easier, and more pleasurable. Within the primary institution of childhood - the family - has deeply and speedily modified. Kids are a lot more independent. They have more opportunities to play with one another, more friends interested in them, other options to explore, trips to take, parents to form same-sex relationships with, grandparents, and other responsible adults who they will see as caretakers. More boys believe in someone to teach them unusual happenings. There's little need to look to the idols of the past. There are more "fatherless" families, maybe for girls also more "motherless" families. "Living in the moment" should lead you through fresh as a one parent and make you sense. Life remains good even if it also remains tough as a one parent.

CHAPTER 3

Nurturing Strong Relationships with Your Children

Remember, it is not only your children who are experiencing new changes. You too can make changes in your role as a parent. Pay attention to your actions and the way you treat your children so that the change is positive. Any increase in time you can get with your children is beneficial. Even if it is only an hour between school and a ball game. No matter how long it takes, turn off your computer at the end of the day or hang up work to be fully invested to hang out with your kids. Encourage them to be ready to share their feelings with you if they are going through difficult situations. Even if you can't be with your kids all the time, letting them know that you are always by their side is something you can do anywhere.

Nurture your relationships with your children. If your children are old enough to talk, they are old enough to get upset by your divorce. They will need to feel loved and supported, so do everything you can to show them that everything is going to be fine. You can avoid a lot of trouble just by talking with them. Cut the lip, "nest here" and "there". Encourage them to share how they feel and talk to them about what you can expect from the future. While doing some things that the whole family used to do together, now conveniently resting with some short lessons. Try teaching your child to play baseball. Go ice skating together on a Friday evening. Doing something new with your child and strengthening your bond with them is important. The family dynamic may be different, but the relationship between you and your child can be improved.

CHAPTER 4

Establishing Routines and Structure

When we walk into a museum, there is an air of structure, calm, and order that's automatically understood. There are defined times for opening and closing that are scrupulously kept; school groups move through their educational experiences in a timely manner; the employees are knowledgeable and respectful. We go to each exhibit in a logical order, not just hopping from room to room or floor to floor in a haphazard fashion. When you go out to dinner, sometimes a reservation is needed. Restaurants have a schedule for when they open and close; you slide into the brown leather booth and know that someone will arrive to take care of your meal. The meal itself will appear in a certain order and the dishes used will appear and disappear several times throughout the course of the experience. It's not something you even have to consciously think about, and that's because it always is the same and feels comfortable. Family life should be no different. In fact, in the next 10 years an organized home will be so sought after that chaos behind closed doors will be seen as a deviation from the norm and an indicator of potential danger.

According to research conducted over the past 20 years, we know that today's kids are more behaviorally impaired than children evaluated in the 1980s. And, while there's certainly no one specific cause, we can make connections between our increasingly chaotic society and the reality that family life is much less structured than it was 25 years ago. With a schedule for each day of the week that's visible and known to every member of the family, individuals can settle comfortably into their roles to help foster an organized life that would otherwise be difficult. Establishing routines is crucial to reducing chaos and promoting healthy mental functioning for all family members. And you don't have to look further than society's most respected public institutions to see the structure and routines that demonstrate and solidify the standards of excellence that we take for granted.

CHAPTER 5

Balancing Work and Family Life

Balancing work and family life is difficult. Throw being a single parent into the mix and it can be borderline impossible. "When you're on your own, it's busy, it's stressful. You've got to try and be in three places at once when you're trying to do all that school-run stuff." Active, successful single parents have just the one pair of hands, so if you are, or know someone who is, wondering how to juggle family and work and still be happy doing it, read on and see how Julya Ashley, single, super mom, managed it. Routine and time management are key concepts that she made use of. "Arranging everything with time is crucial. The breakfast things are ready for the following morning, the clothes are ready for the following morning, so in the morning the only thing I have to do is give breakfast and it's all ready for him, for Simon".

Julya Ashley is a single mom who starts her day at 5 a.m. She grabs a cup of coffee, sits by the window with a book to fill up her soul, and by the time the kids and the nanny are up, she is ready to embrace the hustle and bustle of the day. By the time everyone is out of the house, Ashley has vacuumed, tidied up, and cleared all the toys, so when she gets back home after work, she hasn't got the feeling that "everything is a mess." The whole family home is a happy home. She knows herself and knows her boundaries, so apart from being a teacher, she prefers her side hustle and gets home in time to spend quality time with her children.

CHAPTER 6

Building a Support Network

Worryingly, it seems single parents have balances to strike that the rest of us can't even comprehend. Society expects the worst from single parents, despite the fact they didn't choose their lifestyle. In a society where the odds are stacked against them to begin with, and where there is a real lack of support in the workplace, these parents certainly aren't doing it deliberately, and they shouldn't have to feel guilty for doing the best they can in life. And here's the reality: we all need help, even two-parent families, more often than not. At some point in our lives, we will all be single, whether by choice or circumstance. If others made time to help those single parents, imagine just how much single parents could accomplish. I got the help, and so did many others. Why? Because it takes a village helping to raise great kids.

Leaning on family and friends for support and guidance is critical in the early stages of raising children as a single dad, explains Jason. "I was lucky enough to have people close to me who were always willing and happy to offer advice. I also have a wonderful mother who was always there for me, aunts and uncles who have all played an important role in my children's lives, and a small group of friends that have become like family to us."

CHAPTER 7

Taking Care of Yourself

I say that your kids are the most important person in your life, but it is truly you. So taking care of you is equally as important as spending time with them. As I mentioned in a previous post, you have to set the standard for how you want to be cared for. And the Establishment Phase focuses on you. So, make sure you use your 15 minutes in the morning, pre-kids wake up to center your emotions and set forth a positive tone for the day. Visualization is wonderful in helping you destress and when you find the time to do it, take a bath. Then, at night after the kids are down, take another 15 minutes to center yourself, once again. It is best to end the day as it started, with positivity. These are the standard calming techniques; however, there's also more wholesome activities to choose from if need fits, such as yoga. Find something that best soothes and calms you and invest in that for the best version of yourself. Then, bask in the array of self-appreciation and self-enriching achievements that surround the freshly built, new you.

You can't be a great parent to your kids if you aren't taking care of yourself. Remember when I said to set a great example and catch your reflection in your kids? Well, another part of setting a great example means showing your kids that you take care of yourself too. That means whether you have limited time or not – you must absolutely take at least 30 minutes out of the day to give to yourself; 15 in the morning and 15 at night. I know this is hard and you may feel like you don't have time. Or that it's selfish. But, in all sincerity, it isn't. If you aren't at your absolute best mentally, emotionally, and physically – how can you possibly serve at your absolute best in any other aspect of your life? The answer, in short, is you can't. Because you know full well that anything you do is taken care of with the most important person in your life.

CHAPTER 8

Effective Communication with Co-Parents

Effective communication is crucial when it comes to co-parenting. Effectively convey thoughts and feelings about the past, relate well to co-parents, effectively listen to frustrations, communicate children's challenges, organize care using love and respect, compromise with co-parents, transfer feelings to the appropriate person, and act in compliance with a loving, respectful foundation. None of these tips will help you talk to your ex if you do not want to. If you focus on these elements and approach your ex with loving and respectful attitudes, then that can build the environment of positive, effective co-parenting.

Understanding whose job it is to communicate your feelings and opinions is an essential part of keeping communication collaborative. If your ex would rather not hear your thoughts or opinions, address the issue with a trusted friend or counselor. Keep in mind, much of co-parenting communication can be non-verbal, so take this into consideration. While you're thinking of phrases to say, convey a loving, constructive attitude that will help build positive, effective communication. The following phrases can guide you into communicating positively with your ex-partner.

Effective co-parenting begins with positive communication. It's important to consider the tone, content, context, and form of your communication. The content of your communication should be about the child and should not infringe on the personal lives of you or your ex. The tone and context are equally important, so make sure to communicate with a loving and respectful attitude. Communicate in the form that works best for the situation. There may be times you need to communicate in person and other times through an attorney — think about the context of your communication to determine the most effective channel.

CHAPTER 9

Co-Parenting Strategies for Success

Be mindful of the problems in advance. Communication is an earth-shatteringly difficult topic for most co-parents. However, when communication becomes the basic parental nightmare, parents and children are likely to feel the ease and pride of their carefully wound relations, and suddenly taking a deep breath doesn't seem so hard. In high-emotion situations, remembering the problems and saying "Let's take this offline." This personal note, which you often write to yourself on invoice forms, is incredibly useful. Leaving the conflict where it is and dealing with it elsewhere saves many from the stress of unnecessary problems. It also helps to keep the children calm and relaxed and always works in their favor. Nor did they bring it to the small hearing. (We cannot control other people's behavior, and this would certainly be risky, but we constantly demonstrate to our children the good, and hopefully, with time, they will learn from our example.)

Co-parenting is seldom easy, especially when two parents are trying to manage joint custody and the pressures of shared custody. But some families soon realize that the one-time problem of who will get the children the next weekend has been drastically derailed by an increasingly chaotic school year or conflict resolution nightmare that goes nowhere. As stress increases, children are caught in the middle of an increasing problem. Fortunately, co-parenting can be incredibly successful and surprisingly liberating when both parents can choose to leave a toxic relationship behind (and set healthy boundaries in place) and focus their energy on creating a family oasis for their new life.

CHAPTER 10

Financial Planning and Budgeting

Take stock of your current financial position. Take note of your assets and liabilities. Your net worth can be determined by subtracting your liabilities from your assets. The remainder shows what you have in financial terms. If you are still in the red, then you need to start on the path of becoming liquid, so you can start building financial viability. As your children progress in age, so do their educational needs. Little children may need nursery school fees; primary and secondary school children require fees; and those at the university require more funds and may also possibly need accommodation. And no one can rule out the possibility of having some of the children attending the various levels of school at the same time as they progress in age. A sound plan is to start putting little sums in a special account that will grow without you thinking about it. Use financial instruments like insurance policies and educational policies to keep money aside. When the money is needed for school fees, you pay out instead of borrowing or facing financial stress.

Topics and concepts can be revisited several times, depending on the needs of the individual. Start by clarifying your goal, writing it down, and developing a plan. The goal-setting process should commence with first identifying your values or purpose in life. In the case of couples, it is usually easier to match and synchronize values, aims, and goals, but this may not be so easy with solo parents. For solo parents, make decisions in close relationship with your children, especially decisions that will directly affect them.

CHAPTER 11

Creating a Positive and Loving Environment

It has to do with the rituals, family past occasions, customs, and monuments. While my ex-husband and I separated, our home's climate shattered. This is poor marital lifestyle conditions and lack of self-esteem were intolerable. Our family culture was at its lowest amount, so I was better screen time for my daughter, so men-only and personal tracks, too much studying and PC bowel entertainment. By the time my daughter was six years old, I noticed that this setup was having a really harmful effect on our family. I was given the good gift to take advantage of at least 50% of the time of my daughter and another award to take advantage of all her years looking back at us. To allocate her a pleasantness with our lives together, I was making alterations in our world and focusing on two essential messages. If anything new that you're hoping to have in your life is struggling, concentrate on something else that you value, and the issue that you would like will attentively come to you.

What's a family culture? What is context and family culture? The environment in your house is a pattern of all of your lifestyle that influences your babies, young children, and teens. It's how the little ones feel, from the moment they get home from school until they break the pillows. It addresses how they get dressed, what is in your fridge, how well everyone feels and respects each other, the types of verbal exchanges you have, and how well everyone can function their duties and obligations.

You need to align your environment with your values, beliefs, goals, and dreams. Follow that with the necessary effort to stay true to your heart in every situation. A setting of love, kindness, and happiness to support you in every aspect of your life, and to build a strong family culture that you will all love living with can be nurtured and made better effortlessly over time. All the techniques used to create your environment, or to improve or repair the existing family culture, will build the foundation for your children's fun life.

CHAPTER 12

Teaching Values and Morals

In adding moral values and how to use them pragmatically, there are tasks with negative consequences when they are ignored. For example, stop stealing because it causes harm, learn to respect and obey to avoid being hurt and failing respectively, etc. This is, of course, based on reasonable deductions and not just fear-based commands. Just yesterday, I offered my children more time in front of the TV if they hurt one another senselessly. This is a reward for cooperation and peace dividend. Let them know that when we talk about morality, we are talking about the very essence of life without which everything crumbles. This creates a sense of loss and loss which they should avoid by doing the right things.

Values are not about whom your children marry in the future or whether or not they will steal from great grandma's retirement fund. They are about the things that make life much more enjoyable and meaningful. Then talk about them in the abstract and even oppose certain ones at the right time. Some may argue that the emphasis on personal freedoms and rights by Western societies has suffocated the sense of community in the East. For example, rights have been placed above duties to country and society. It is the job of every parent to teach their children the importance of balance and informed choice. This is what will make them happy, wholesome, and fulfilled people.

Knowing what matters to you and setting clear boundaries is critical. These are the rules of your life and your home. Values are those things that you can teach and mold through example. Try things like showing kindness to others, even better if it comes at a time when no one is watching. Ask the question, "When I am not with you, would you show kindness to others?" Their response will tell you how much they learned from your example. Now ask them, "If you learn how to challenge yourself more, would you grow and become a happy person?" Offer them a time with no chores if you hear the word "powerless" in the kitchen. This makes them think about what they want by way of power at home and in life. The best time to do this is as they help, which is another learning opportunity.

CHAPTER 13

Encouraging Independence and Responsibility

This task cannot be achieved overnight. Now that your family is almost perfect, it may be time to put in place a chore chart. Each child is responsible for his or her own needs, such as clothes and personal effects. Younger children may need more time to complete their tasks than older children. For example, a seven-year-old may need 10 to 15 minutes to clean up his or her room, while a 12-year-old may need 5 to 10 minutes. Younger children can also be paired with older children to clean their room. This is also a time for building bridges and for sharing a moment of complicity between brothers and sisters. In addition, the older child can also act as a role model and teach the younger child how to make the task easier.

One of the challenges of assuming the role of both parents is finding the balance between hovering over the children and the need to maintain control over the household at the very same time. After all, part of growing up involves taking on more and more responsibility. When children never or barely get the chance to demonstrate this, they risk not ever being allowed to grow up. The formed need to tend to those who have not fully, if at all, developed the necessary skills to be well on their own almost prevents their children from doing this. Therefore, a big part of one-parent households is remembering and making a conscious effort to push the kids to take care of themselves and their share of the household.

CHAPTER 14

Helping Children Cope with Divorce or Separation

To help children follow divorce or separation, parents can provide children with proper facilities, understand their point of view, and take help from friends and family. Parents should understand children's emotions, come to their level of understanding, and speak realistically about a parent's decision. Parents should make themselves friendly with each other and provide children varied opportunities to spend time with each parent. It should be done in an open and understanding manner towards married parents. Married parents should consider separating as a last option because in a married relationship too, the bond and responsibility of parenthood is far greater and permanent than that of marital life. Moreover, separations and divorce not only affect the personality but also degrade the morale of children. The psychological trauma of divorce is harder than the loss of a spouse.

Changes in the family can be very stressful and unsettling for children. It is normal for a period of adjustment to take place wherever a child spends time following a separation. It is only natural for parents to worry that changes to the family group and their routine will have a negative impact on their children. There are many factors which can affect what that impact – including the parents' relationship and ability to cooperate, how well children are supported, the duration of the separation, the individuality of the child, and the age at which the changes take place. If the relationship between parents settles down positively after the initial angst and sometime for acceptance and acclimatization to the new situation, parents can be reassured that most separations do not have a long-term harmful impact.

CHAPTER 15

Dealing with Behavioral Challenges

For when the misbehaving occurs, a single parent should restate an inappropriate behavior, and if needed, immediately issue a directive concerning how to behave to fix the problem. A key step to breaking up the child's bad behavior is to issue a serious directive, delivered with strong language to get the child's attention, and to get their attention and center their negative feelings. As they are successful in attracting the child's attention, they have to keep using strong language to impress the force of the lecture. The child should then have to act responsibly when they've answered correctly — as long as they have the maturity to do so. But, if it is a single parent dealing with an impatient young child with a lack of focus and maturity, then a single parent should know that the child has not yet developed enough responsibility nor do they have the ability to control their behavior quite yet.

Dealing with toddlers and younger kids who throw tantrums can be stressful for any parent, but singles and single parents who constantly deal with unreasonable bad behavior need a strategy of planning and developing a plan of actions to effectively manage their child's conduct. A single parent should plan initial steps when future problems occur so that they will be more confident about how to handle children's unacceptable behavior. It is usually necessary to use training and behavioral techniques to teach the children to behave when they are not at their best. With new behavior problems, the first step is for the single parent to evaluate the situation, and then prepare a plan of actions before actual problems occur. With advanced planning, one will be quick to develop an acceptable behavior in negative situations. When one is well-prepared for the individual problems that are frequently occurring, it will not be possible to find the most effective, immediately occurring techniques.

CHAPTER 16

Promoting Education and Academic Success

In some families, parents start thinking about their children's education when they are still babies. But sometimes this is not the case, such as in the single-parent family that I portrayed earlier in this text, where education can become more of a serious topic after the children have already reached school age. I still remember the sincere concern voiced by the previously mentioned mother about her children's future when, in the interview, she said the following: "I think mostly about how I could advance the studies of my kids." Despite formal education having previously been seen as something that was not necessarily important for my interviewed character, at some point in her life, the loss of her life partner made her worried enough to search for great advancements in her children's studies. She even stated her non-negotiable decision to send her children to a private school, the Teachers Cooperative that would provide the best guidance for them. Through conflicts and sacrifices that had to be made to work hard on her own, she managed to discover ways and put together conditions to approximate the potential of her two young girls and her boy to bring about the highest degree of academic success possible.

Your children's academic achievement is one of the most important determining factors in ensuring their long-term success. High marks in school (and later, in university) can open doors to new opportunities, help your children realize their full potential and expand their horizons, turning them into successful and productive citizens with healthy lifestyles and happy personalities. Promoting your children's education is not just the responsibility of their schools and teachers. Your influence as a parent is much more crucial in determining your children's academic success than family background factors, such as social class, ethnicity and family size, as well as parental attitudes and aspirations for the education of their children. Even when you have to be a single parent, as is the case described in the paragraphs that will now follow, it is up to you to motivate children, plan their educational activities and prioritize questions related to their studies.

CHAPTER 17

Fostering Emotional Well-being

We must protect ourselves and our children by giving attention to the needs we possess, both in presence and absence of serious traumatic events. Only by supporting well-being today do we conceptually recover losses of support sustained in the past. Acknowledge personal experiences with the same compassion one would extend to another. We must be whole within in order to truly live, and have whole relationships. We must be open to solutions that present and live within them each day. Our life's blueprint becomes designed through our thoughts and prayers in action. Practice. Always strive to understand the woman, man or child. Believe in our collective power to work with these angels who serve tirelessly. We are all precious, priceless gifts of the Divine – we are here to love, share our joys and sorrows, console and heal.

Within a recovering population, emotional well-being is absent. Poorly-equipped adults demonstrate little emotion, as they attempt to emotionally repair themselves while their children live aching for comforting attention of a consciously-aware mother or father who actually sees them. Children perpetually confined to their rooms cling to visions of better times and heal themselves. In a cruel twister of fate, should an incapacitated parent recover emotionally, they find their children, absent in spirit with no wish to return. To not witness what the avoidance of personal and family needs produces in these 'hopes' one can only distinguish logical computations at work. No mother or father can survive for any serious length of time and have a relationship with their child where emotional needs are ignored.

CHAPTER 18

Strengthening Sibling Bonds

There is something magical and unique in the way they are close, the way they know when the other is not fine, and wanting to help. The magical bond that one sibling has with the other does not arise from the exact same experience of loss. There are nuances to the feelings that are easy to understand for one who goes through it. First of all, we are dealing with individuals from the same family, so we have many characteristics in common. Second, the experience of loss is, although similar, completely subjective, and for that reason alone there are no two feelings around the subject that are exactly the same. And the closest to family support, the stronger and more cohesive the bond between brothers. The gap between siblings when the lone support is always the parent. Faced with so much affection and the consequences of the divorce, my children respect each other. The one who saw the pain of the other in the rupture of our family knows how to give empathy, concern, and support to the brother when the other experiences any setback in their daily lives.

The divorce of a parent can have a huge impact on siblings. The shared experience of two people who grew up in the same house with parents who are no longer together can be intense. The disconnect that the parent often experiences affects the siblings. It is normal for them to go through stages of sadness, distraction, confusion, anger, anguish, and other emotions through the process of the rupture of the family unit. The opportunities for them to learn from each other about how to handle each of those stages are immense. Three months after my divorce, our three children lived a typical full day and the baby asked, "Am I the only one who still misses Dad?" Ten minutes later, my daughter confessed that she had not seen our relationship with the same eyes as her brother and that my sadness made her feel more intense than him. I held back my tears and requested that I get empathy in such a deep expression of my children.

CHAPTER 19

Fun and Bonding Activities for the Family

For families that like reading, reading bedtime stories together can be a great way for family members to find time to interact. As they share and discuss the narrative, memorable moments can be created that will stay with the family for their entire life. No matter how old they are, children remember the bedtime stories, especially when their parents take time to act out their parts with enthusiasm. The idea of reenacting favorite scenes can make the grooming rituals just another doorway to building their lasting bonds. Family members can create even richer memories by piling into their vehicles and taking long road trips that can be family bonding journeys at the same time. Creating long-lasting memories by driving on rural roads and exploring nature in camping grounds and resorts will ensure their children will have plenty to smile about at dinnertime. If a long road trip is too difficult, families can also take short road trips instead. One parent has said that a road trip to a distant city can definitely create memories that could last well into adulthood.

There are many fun things for families to do together, and to choose just ten to be best would be arguably unfair. Therefore, here are simply some fun things that families can do to help bond and also genuinely have fun with each other. Before family activities can truly happen, you have to decide as a family to do them. Your children must be turned down the idea of playing video games, watching TV, and aimlessly using their personal computing devices in favor of creating living and rich memories with their family. Once you get them onboard, here are 20 things that you can consider. Sure this sounds corny, but it is as old as time: taking family walks allows the members to enjoy each other's company, converse, and at the same time allows everyone to remain active. Take time to explore local parks and trails, so the walks are varied and fun for everyone. Getting exercise benefits the whole family, so the walks are a good family activity in every way.

CHAPTER 20

Celebrating Milestones and Special Occasions

For all the milestones one lives through with your kids, also remember to create memories of your family unit, alone. Sometimes we celebrate first-year birthday parties, graduations, and holidays twice. At other moments, alone, we surrender to the joy of living our special occasion with the family unit that is present. This is positive and important. Holidays, such as birthdays, Mother's Day, and Father's Day can present themselves as a bitter drink to the parent who lives without the help and support of the other, but they can also give off a delicious taste of pure love if you choose for a softened gaze on the situation. You are both the mom and the dad at the same time. You deserve to make a beautiful party in your own honor. Celebrating, either with children, family, or friends, will create a happy memory giving you the certainty of the effective and affectionate mother/father you are.

Explain to your children that a new way to do things does not mean that the things they fantasize or dream about with the other parent lose meaning. Show your kids that you also celebrate the other family in their absences through acts of love and hope. Teach them, through music, drawing, writing, or perhaps getting involved with your neighbors who might be missing something, that love is always welcomed, in all its forms. I made poems for the kids and placed them in their backpacks on the days they had to be with the other parent. I learned the importance of hidden notes to make love last.

CHAPTER 21

Managing Stress and Burnout

I recently found out that you don't have to be married nor do you have to be a single parent to experience symptoms of burnout. Symptoms such as those of chronic fatigue (such as sleeping and not feeling rested), feeling kind of forgetful (like where did I set my cup of coffee again?), always to most of the time feeling like you have no control, being occupied with your children, and just simply being tired. My doctor asked if I lived in an area with mold (not really), if I was losing too much sleep due to waking up from noises at night (a little, yes), and what type of work I did (I have been taking care of foster children). Well, according to my doctor, symptoms of chronic fatigue are based on our deep emotions. She takes this information and runs with it. Wild, huh? I am able to think clearly about it all now. Doc stated that when you are not thinking clearly, you feel like you're in an accident when you are not (things appear to be moving extremely slow and you feel like you are moving super fast), and you start to question yourself on the most mundane things.

The stress of work, single parenting, and state assistance brings me to tears sometimes. It's difficult to admit because I want to be stronger than that, but sometimes I think about the things that I want and feel sorry for myself. Then, I focus on something else and move past it for the time being. And sometimes those tears are what I need to release the stress that has built up. Stress is normal when you are in a position that God never intended for us to be in, but the problem comes when it starts to cause health problems. We've all heard the stories of people who have died of a heart attack or stroke because they allowed their stress to consume them. You have to allow yourself to cry, walk away from whatever is causing the stress, and find time to release the tension.

CHAPTER 22

Seeking Professional Help and Counseling

Professional counselors can provide sound advice and support for all kinds of single parents. Kids of all ages can open up about their feelings with adults that have the skills of talking to children and getting them to talk about their worries, anger and fears. In contrast to what they see in fairy tales and read in the best novels, Moy argues that all families are real and their quality comes from being connected. A family member, even if it's just one, can make a house a home. Therefore, it's very important for those sitting in the painful chairs to seek professional help, like counseling, without fear or without being embarrassed about solo parenting choices. No need to wait until everything falls apart.

One of the smaller changes brought on by my split is that I'm automatically a single parent now. Even when I'm with my kids and my ex calls to talk to them over the phone, they know which parent they're talking to. Making quick decisions for my kids or changing a plan as I see fit doesn't require that I look for a partner with which to confirm a good parenting move. While sharing the weight of parenting can be invaluable in many ways, just as often we appreciate the fewer boundaries and faster pace at which decisions are made when we're parenting solo. After keeping up with two kids day-in and day-out though, I admit that I'm feeling spent, and like parenting – juggling kids, emotions, activities, schedules – is just too much. I'm not really sure which life changes are best to free up more time, because I can't let go of any of them. What can I do?

CHAPTER 23

Embracing Change and Adapting to New Circumstances

I understand the need in this globally competitive society to continually grow and overcome challenges. However, I'm also working to develop a new success storyline for solo parents, which focuses on personal growth and self-recognition, not the fairness of society or limitations. This is because, in comparison to our parenting nation, single parents stand alone and the judgments can lump us into an inflexible living situation. The number of dependents or societal redistricting is gone. Supporting one another, we build our own networks of help that are acknowledged to help us navigate and empower family life. Thus, we move beyond any societal assumptions, stereotypes, and statistics and live in the present by embracing change. Nothing will change until we change ourselves and our assumptions to open our hearts and minds. When setting preferences for a happy home solo, the little kid in us comes out to acknowledge that we are different, embracing the uniqueness of our family lifestyles. Now, as we start to develop our common identity and voice, connecting it to world change, we can boldly chart a new success story and ensure thereby that life will offer to ourselves and our young accidents.

Albert Einstein is often quoted as stating, "The definition of insanity is doing the same things over and over and expecting different results." This sentiment suggests that growth involves changing our behavior instead of waiting for people and circumstances to change. Despite the desire for things to happen and people to change and grow to be more like what we want, positive change always begins in us when we open ourselves to new possibilities and experiences. We need to stop playing the comparative value game with others while avoiding viewing ourselves as nothing more than a global society's wardrobe malfunction.

CHAPTER 24

Exploring Co-Parenting Apps and Tools

Before, during, and after having a kid, it can be all cake and wine with sentiment about replacing this family photo project that used to only have a takeout box. On one hand, we believe divorcing parents say the wrong things and get their kids in a tizzy because they allow their kids to see/hear the fighting and then similarly blame no-longer-in-love parents for raising takeout-serving self-absorbed kids. We have long agreed that using tools made specifically for parents to communicate so kids don't witness the dolt duo fail can only be a golden idea. This feels like a truth we got out of basics coach on track to board the first big yellow turkey pavilion that Rhodes pianostodno. Buried in "woo sh*t you said to an eight-year-old," are plenty of what-could-be treasures for any parent who could use help from the starting lineup. While recording those gems/meltdowns in a convenient notebook that also helps Vivitars, United Pros, and Kathlynn relax, point cards, and smart dog treats.

When you're the only parent in the home, you're definitely doing the management, but are you managing the partnership well? Co-parenting is about the business of raising a child together, and from the standpoint of management, even if you are the only parent in the home, your job is still to get the help you need to raise a human that will be a happy and responsible addition to society (one who doesn't move back in with you). While this is your job, you will also have ample opportunities to be a hypocrite or a wordsmith or a workhorse or a whiner or an all-star. With all that and the guilt and the joy, single parenting is a crazy fun not-so-fun job where faith, the right two feet, and nagging your own mother really do move the mountains you make. And as much as some of the co-parenting app-based tools on the slide may be marketed to help never-married and separated parents, the simple fact is, when you are the only parent in the house, you're the one who's doing it all and doing it all the time.

CHAPTER 25

Single Parenting and Dating

The thought of dating can be as frightening as dating itself. In Single Parenthood and Dating, Know Where You're Coming From, Know Where You're Going, and also Know What You're Looking For, mother Kathleen Lellion writes "The Charmer", her first piece of fiction. She advises to consider what you deemed important when dating before. Also maintain or gain an understanding into your dating style, such as casual and overprotective or a "do-over" parent, initiating intense relationships that are "the exact wrong thing at this time". By doing so, a single parent dating can secure relationships that "fight new codes of superficiality" and nurture meaningful bonds that are open with a greater depth of conversation and preparedness for the moves and level of involvement that could possibly occur.

The Family Circle magazine article advises that single parents often find it difficult to be away from their children and may feel guilty about leaving them. While that sentiment is common, it is critical that you feed your personal life. Your social life feeds your spirit, and laughter can do more than nourish your soul, it can truly help soothe your life's struggle. You can ease worries about children and exchange babysitting with friends. You may also have the option of making time with a new friend a family event, allowing your children to participate, easing guilt and also making for a gentle stride toward independence. Children need to know that it is healthy and natural for parents to rely on others, and collaborative family activities can provide comfort to children, as well as build strong bonds between you and your children's caretakers. If children feel secure, they are better able to accept changes and support your well-being.

CHAPTER 26

Dealing with Parental Guilt

Concern for your children is a universal feature of parenthood and is the most difficult issue separating single from two-parent homes. As parents, we all try to get our children to their full potential, exhibit caring, love, and understanding, listen intently, and be careful with our words, expressions, and most importantly, our reactions. When your child is upset, tell them you understand the seriousness of the situation and provide an answer to the problem if you're able. Occupying your time with your children when you need alone time can lead to displaying discontent, impatience, and neglect for your child, which can then result in a lack of enthusiasm and lack of security. We are human and make mistakes and have our own selfish desires. Misjudgments and harmful responses are inevitable. But the grace we exhibit when we forgive and love cleanses the heart from hurt and voids, which strengthens our relationship. Parental guilt seeks to harm, wound, and imprison. Be contented with healthy emotional and responsible release.

Treating myself like I treat others can be the key to my healing. Verbal and psychological abuse from others, and indeed self-abuse, should no longer be acceptable or tolerated. I often worry about not being enough, that I'm not doing enough, or doing things correctly. I also worry about what error I am making in regards to my parenting.

Unfortunately, I have learned that letting my feelings of guilt dishonor myself, and sometimes others, comes easy as a billowing breeze. But the myth of "perfect" anything, especially a family, should not be followed or pursued.

CHAPTER 27

Setting Boundaries and Discipline Strategies

Many bad decisions arise when a teen is following a group behavior instead of his (or her) own internal guidelines, when he is afraid of appearing to be foolish or weak in front of peers, and when he's enticed by a pleasurable impulse. It should be said that focusing on the self forms a sound adult who's less likely to follow or engage in group situations that would get him in trouble initially. For example, a party presents many opportunities for other like-age drinkers and pressure to do what others are doing, but if a teen is in close "connection" with his parents and has an internal need to stay on his chosen path, he will be much more likely to appreciate the value of a path that excludes following a peer-based group homogeneity. The tendency might arise years later, if at all, when he's questioning his choices independently, or when he tries to rationalize them to other people. Setting boundaries with small children can be easier because of the limited opportunity for antisocial behaviors, but it is important that kids know who is in charge. Collect a library of discipline strategies; for some considerations refer back to the section on society and the role-models provided for the child. Remember, discipline is there to bound the environment to keep the child safe while he develops into a social member. Discovery of acceptable social limits is the ultimate goal in disciplining a young person. Attitude, behavior, and protocol roll downhill, break the cycle with autonomous individuals. Build relationships and family with respect and integrity. Stand firm but fair always. Treat other people as you would like to be treated in everyday encounters and larger life choices. Different views on punctuality, respect, and attitudes of judgment are arbitrary and therefore are not fair components of discipline, but constructively focusing on the intended result(s) of the desired behaviors is a significant tool. Patient discipline is effective because a child relatively self-disciplines earlier, learns to process the benefits of his behavior and the consequences of his actions. In my house, negative aspects of behavior are greatly minimized and periodic emphasis on the clear benefit of your choices has helped to create well-behaved, thoughtful children.

Setting boundaries is a challenge for any parent, particularly if you are setting them alone. Social comparisons with traditionally raised groups will make you question if you have made the right choices. It is important to remain focused on the fundamentals and underlying principles as you create your own unique parenting strategies. Consider the kind of adult you want your child to become and then define the boundaries to move him in that direction. Getting support from other parents who share similar values and resources that have the same goals is important to maintain confidence in your parenting choices. This will be particularly important when you are feeling tired, overworked, or disheartened. It is common for a parent to be excited about implementing new ideas, but a partner tends to notice if something isn't working and will help you to bring other creative ideas into play to avoid burnout. Remind teenagers of their capacity to reason, their decision-making responsibilities, and explain why you are concerned about a situation. This helps them to understand your reasoning and engage in problem-solving, both of which contribute to creating a mature young person who is capable of making smart decisions on his own.

CHAPTER 28

Encouraging Open Communication with Your Children

When things get so bad that open communication halts, involving a counselor may help (even prevent). I see this as similar to a health check-up. Kids have many and varied communication needs; figure out how to meet these needs in your home. It's also important to teach how to better understand others who communicate in other natural (for them) ways. This is covered more in point 15, The Elephant in Communication: Teaching Parenting Styles and Multiple Intelligence. Especially when communication does not come easily to them, consider our children are never more deserving of our caring oversight and respect than now.

Understand your children's communication needs. Some kids are more naturally chatty than others, and there are lots of factors which create these natural styles. During your conversations, keep what research shows kids want rear in mind – in some cases, it could mean sharing more about your own life. It's difficult for kids when you protect them by saying you are okay when you are not. It bothers them when they are not able to express an emotion none of their friends ever have. Share what you felt like when you were their age. (I've done this, even when they were more frightened than I expected.) And listen to them. Rumors continue kids tell peers more about themselves than they share with us – so let's add to (not replace) these conversations by asking about their days and really caring what they share.

CHAPTER 29

Promoting Healthy Habits and Self-Care

Time out. Practice good hygiene, aim to look good, and dress well, and as much as possible, without spending beyond your means. Your kids will learn the value of cleanliness and neatness. They will learn to take pride in their appearance and not be shy to present themselves properly in any situation. Your behavior and example will show them that appearance is important because it impacts self-esteem and confidence. They will inculcate their own sense of style and image. At the end of the day, they will emulate you, without compromising their individuality. Your partner should also do this, as he also plays a vital role in shaping his children's self-esteem. The science behind this is "mirror neurons" which are described by some psychologists as "Monkey See, Monkey Do". We emulate behaviors and express emotions of others.

Health is wealth. Keep your family healthy. Help them develop healthy eating habits and instill the importance of cleanliness and dental hygiene, especially because oral health is linked to various systemic conditions. Keep illnesses at bay by ensuring that the family practices proper nutrition, exercises regularly, and gets sufficient sleep. Set a good example by practicing what you preach. You'll also save more, even if you're a single mom, with fewer visits to the doctor.

CHAPTER 30

Building Resilience in Your Children

For most families, divorce leads the list of challenging situations your children will face. Model sure and cheerful concern for your children's reactions. Help them navigate between the two homes they may now have. Be especially alert to their feelings of "belonging" and what may be "doubles" - a pair that doesn't match, parents that practice different rules - and help them sort out those in a way where neither feels victimized. No discipline should be lightened to "make up for" a single-parent home. It is a powerful mark of encouragement and of hope to the inner being, to believe they can meet the same rules as before. Aside from possible health reasons, they can, and doing so helps make their world a predictable and hence a safer one. The safe environment and the cohesiveness of the single-parent home may be one of the strengths of a family that contributes to the development of the respect and empathy that mark resilient individuals.

Even in the happiest and best of homes, children need help developing resilience. Building resilience is just another word for taking your children with you as you model flexibility, love, perseverance, and cognitive willingness to find the best in a difficult situation. Additionally, special to children of one-parent families is the need to also help them understand what is going on - first as they adjust to their initial loss, and second, as they grow and encounter differences between their situation and that of children in two-parent families.

CHAPTER 31

Finding Joy and Happiness in Single Parenthood

Understanding happiness this way accounts for how single parents (no matter how hard their lives) can be happy. They can also keep their children happy, despite the "incomplete" family configuration. Single-parent families are deprived of what are often considered ideal circumstances. Thereby, deprived children inevitably feel lacking, or at least confused about families that become easy and natural matters for other children. Suleman's 14 children could be different; 8 of them were already twins before three other children were born. Such success is difficult to deal with even by single parents who are as fortunate as Suleman and as wealthy as. Relations and communications are not only complex but also emotionally risky. Former spouses can easily instruct the children against their own parents. Moreover, during emotional hunting, children often suffer the loss of ordinary care and logic, which can lead them further on the wrong track. Emotion can emotionally kill children, but good emotions can also build the final happiness of a single family.

In the absence of America's most famous single parent, Suleman's 14 children did not seem to differ from other children living in two-parent households. It turns out, human resilience even applies to both single parents and large families. Moreover, one of the first people to call

Suleman was her own mother. If you are the only parent in your family, this is good news. Single parents can be a big happy family. Understand the following about happiness. Happiness and life satisfaction are often related, but different. Although feeling happy is a sign of life satisfaction at that time, this feeling is transitory. Someone who has high life satisfaction feels happy up and down, but maintains a stable mood after happiness or pleasure. Happiness arises from the emotions of joy, while life satisfaction tends to be long-lasting derived from healthy and strong passion and interests, such as relationships, work, or hobbies that foster self-achievement for individuals.

CHAPTER 32

Conclusion

That said, single parenting is not ideal. The marriage of our parents, or that of another family, is ideal. Regardless of the nature of the parenting design, we have a Creator who loves us and addresses our needs appropriately. And we have one another. Like widows - hearts and hands prizing and praying for the families of neighbors, we single parents have much to offer. Never forget: this one parent reality of your family is not by chance. It has been the intent of our heavenly Parent for you to be whole. Embrace His plan. The balance that you can leverage in parenting, with many of the qualities reviewed in previous chapters, can be discovered in Him. This is the surest route to happiness in the now and always.

Becoming a single parent through the process of divorce, adoption, or dating - whatever the cause - can be overwhelming. But God's design for the family is a great comfort! Neither marriage - partnership between Adam and Eve - nor family solohood - motherless Baby Jesus under the watch of Joseph - are constructs of humanity. Instead, from this beginning to the end in the Book of Revelation where we see the bride of Jesus as the church, a community of single-and-married people, the family is a gift of God. Not surprisingly, when single, He does enable us to do everything we need to do. We have a role of both father and mother inherent in the physiological design of the human.